Mandala Coloring Book V.5

Sparks Creativity

Andrea T. Cross

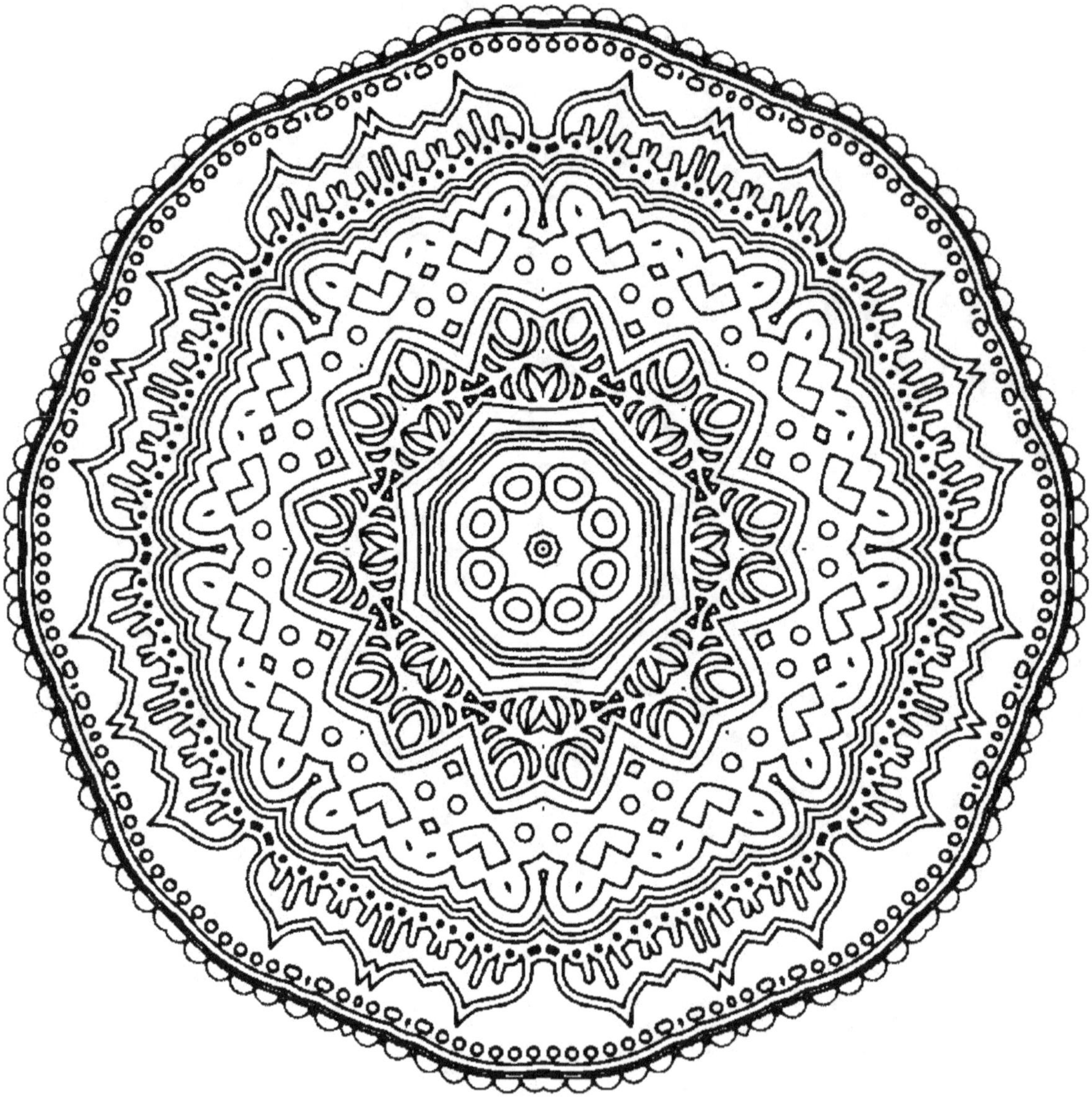

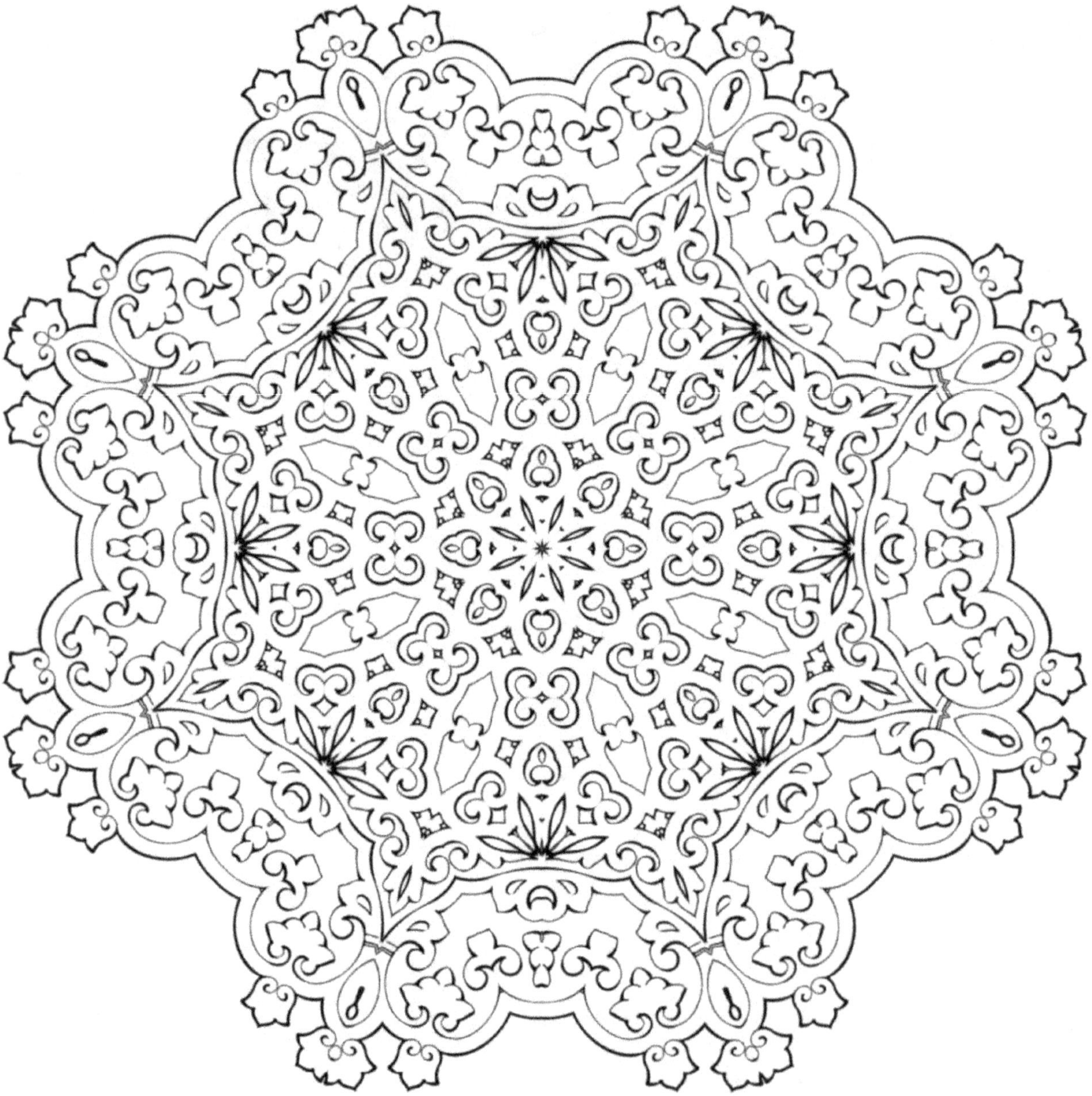

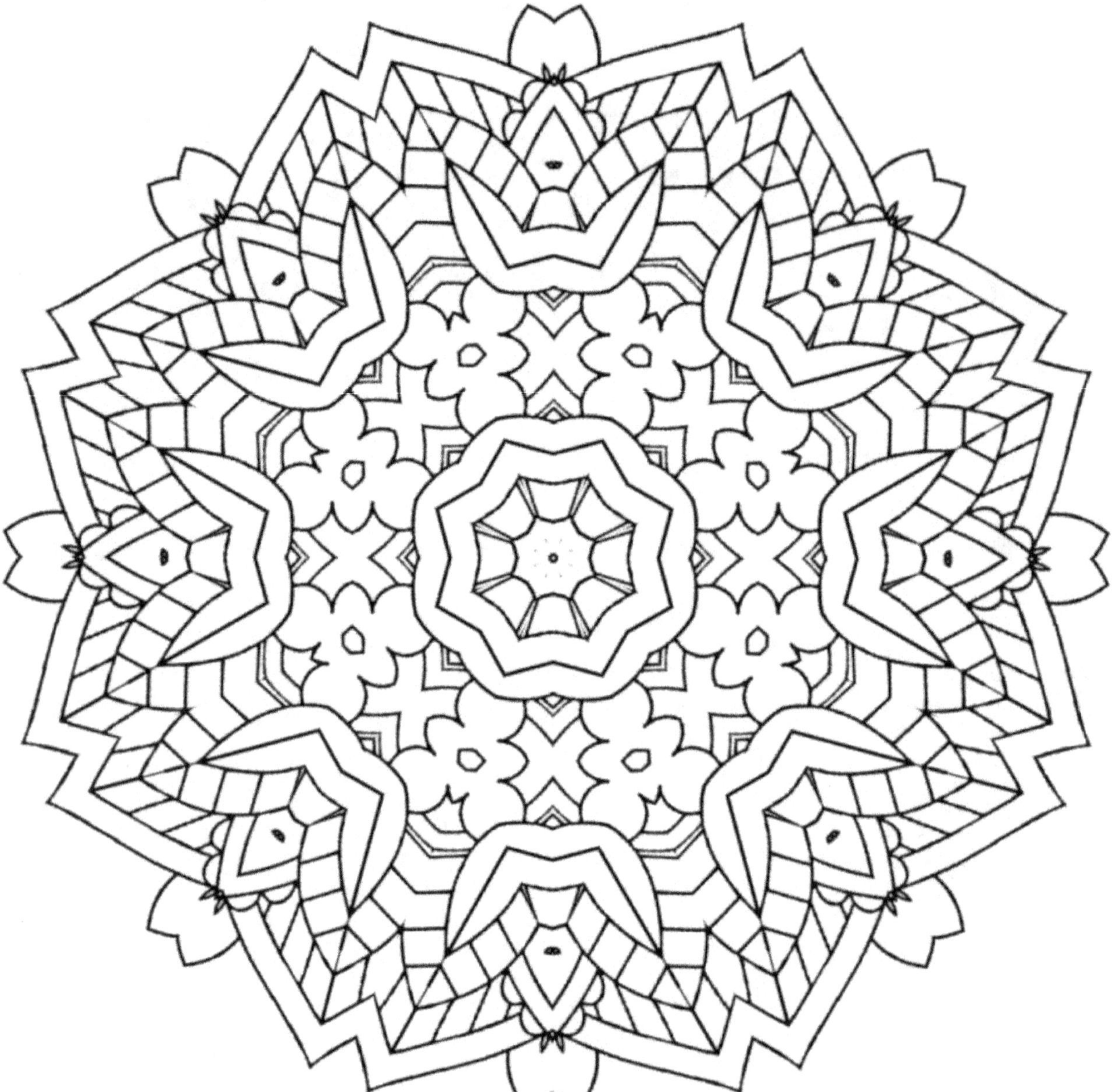

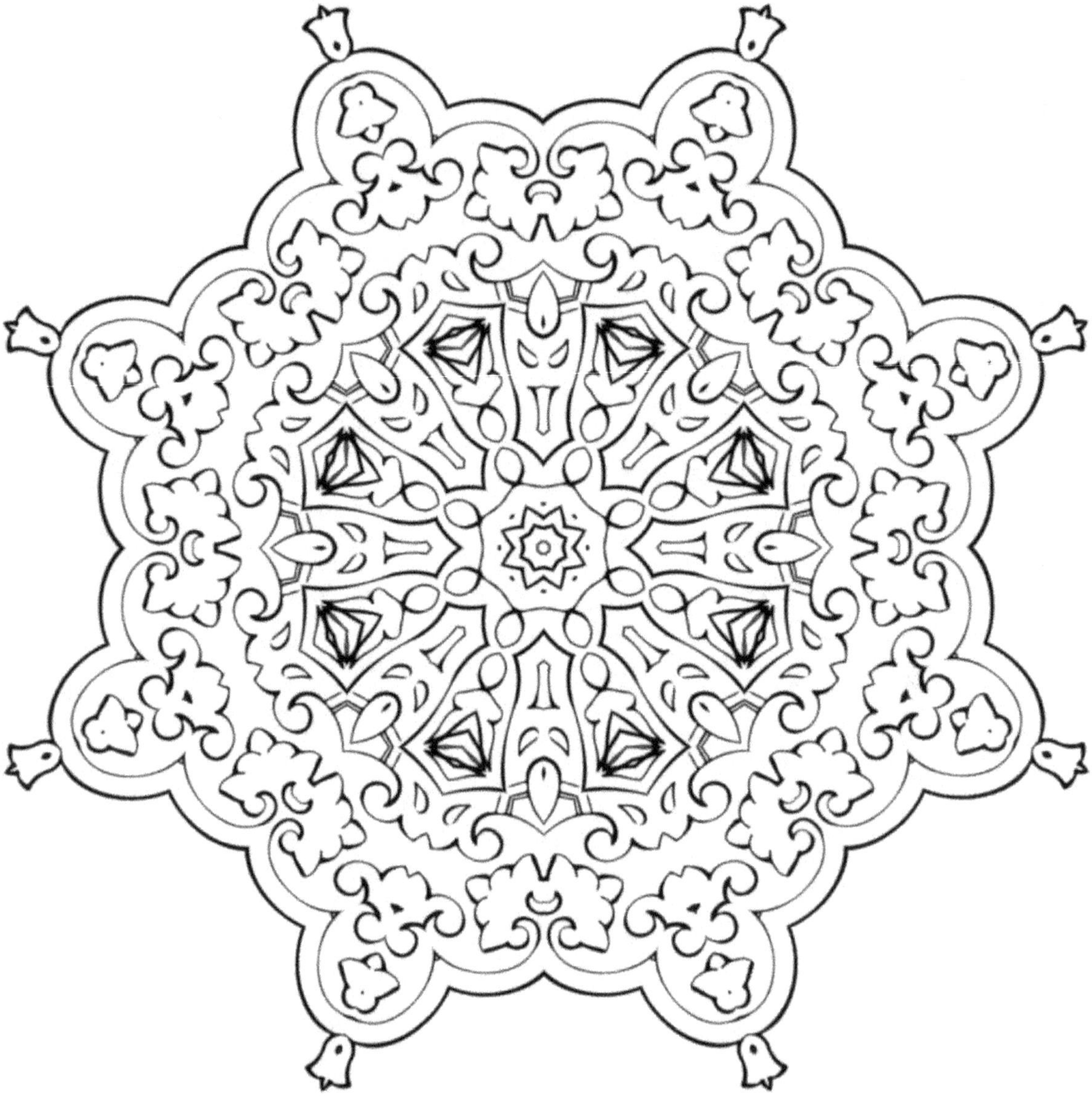

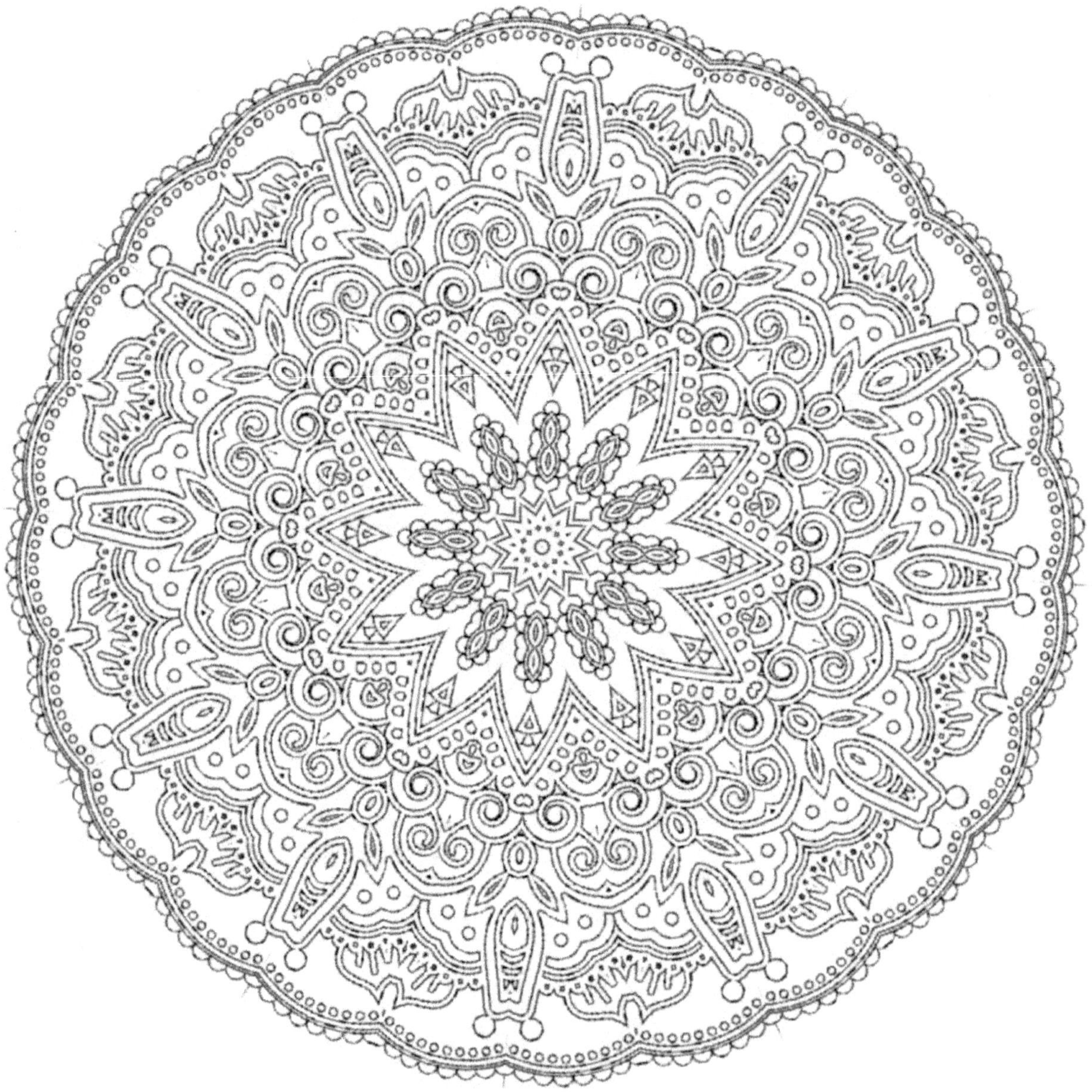

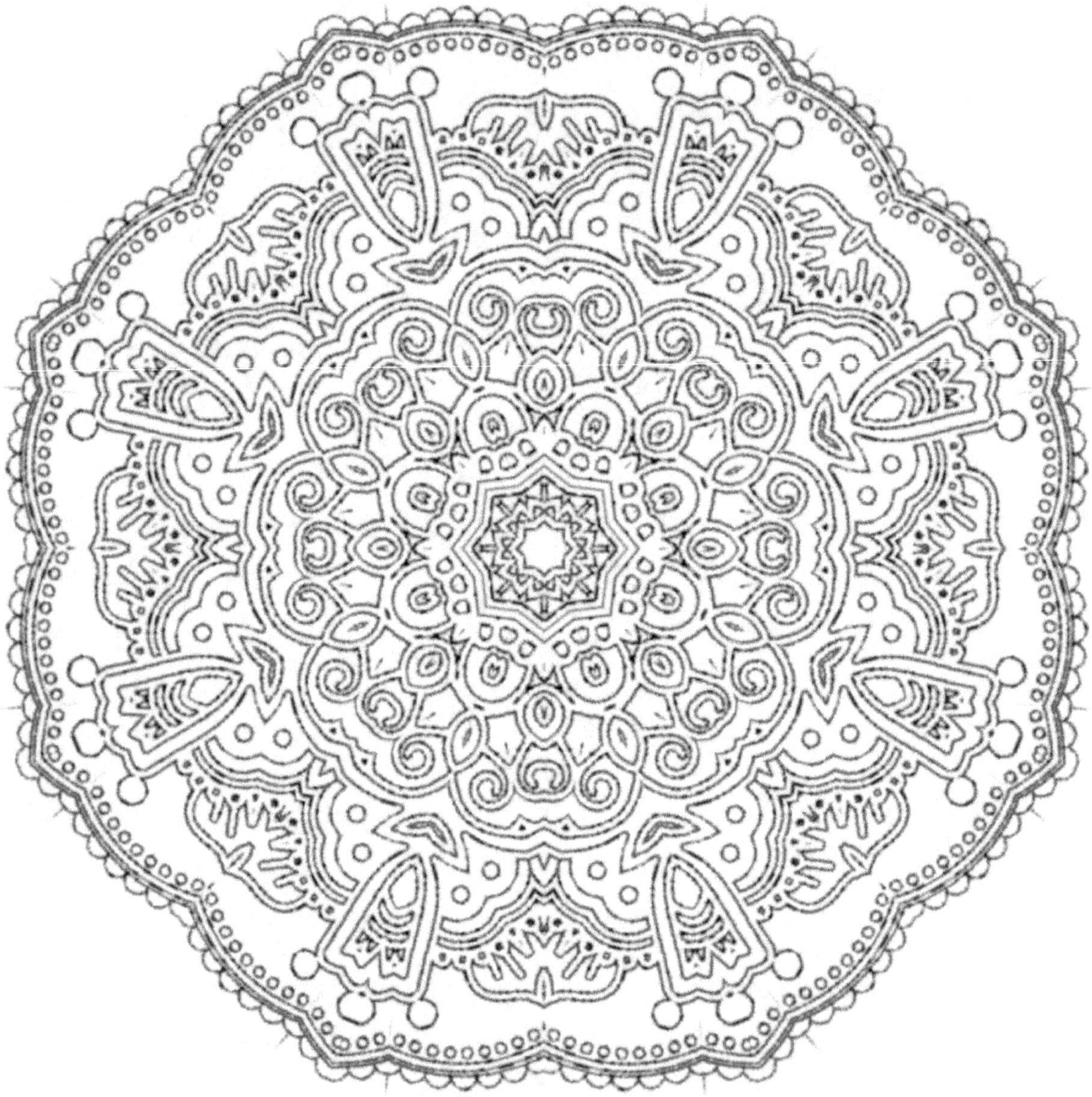

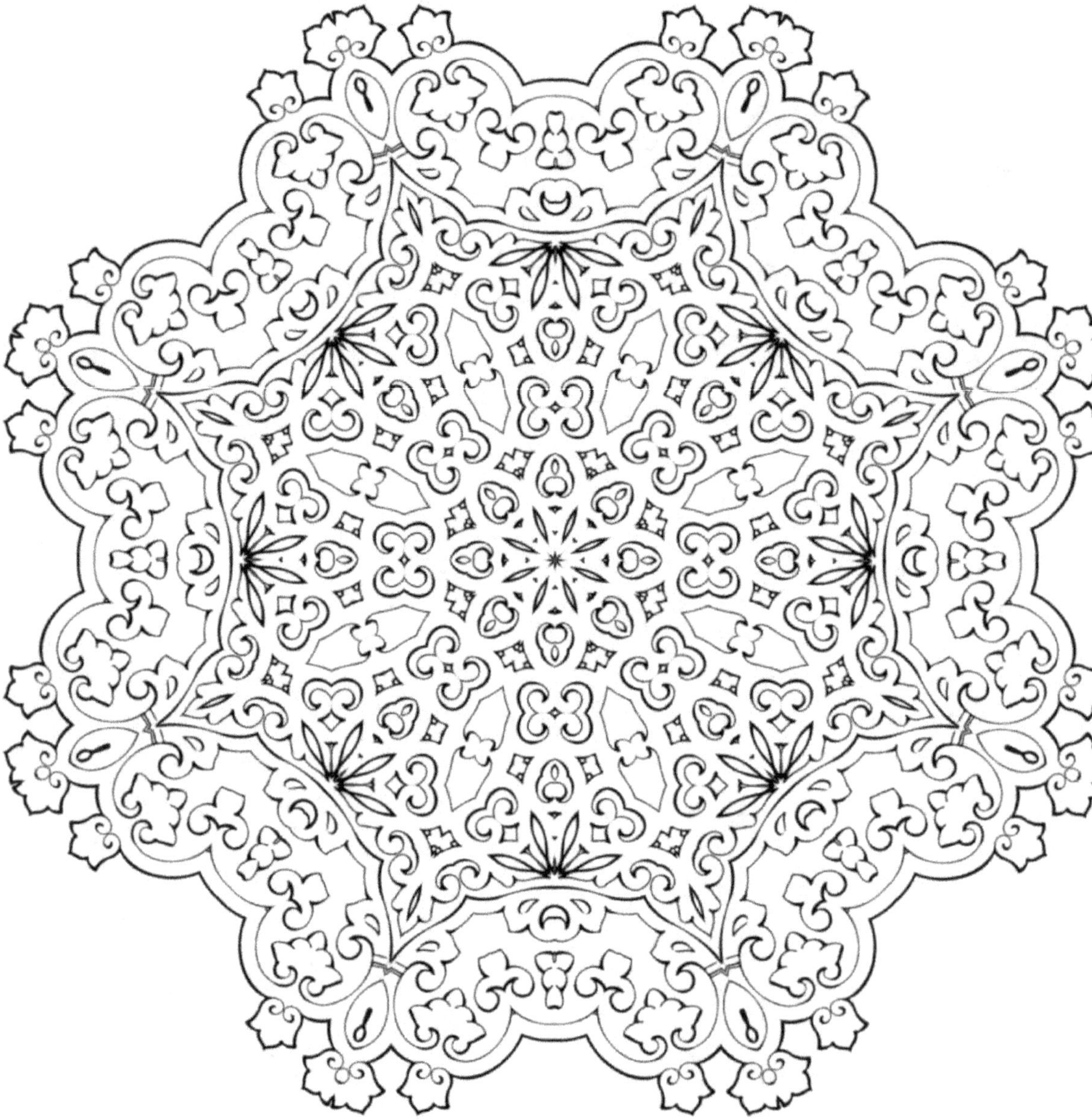

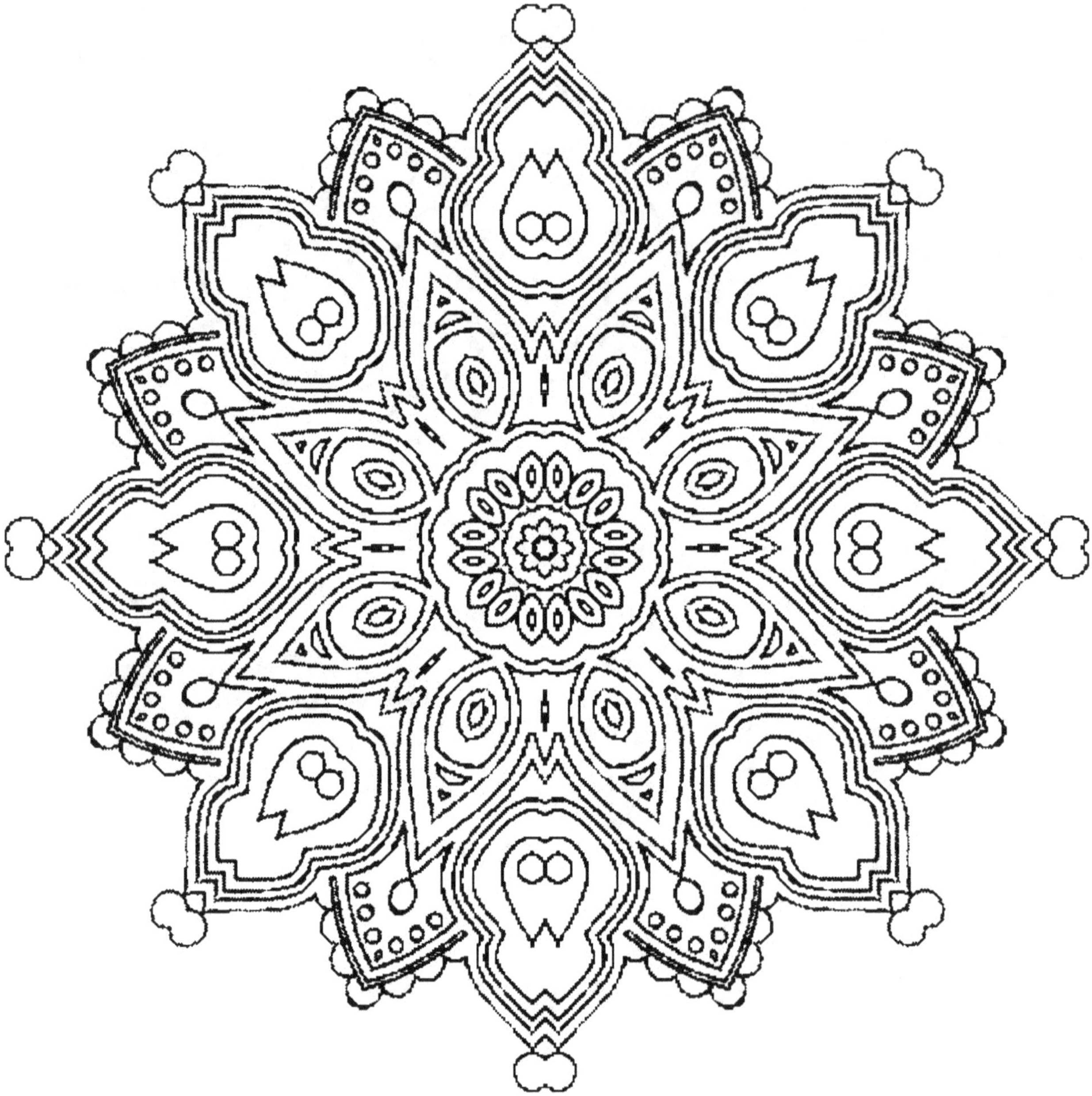

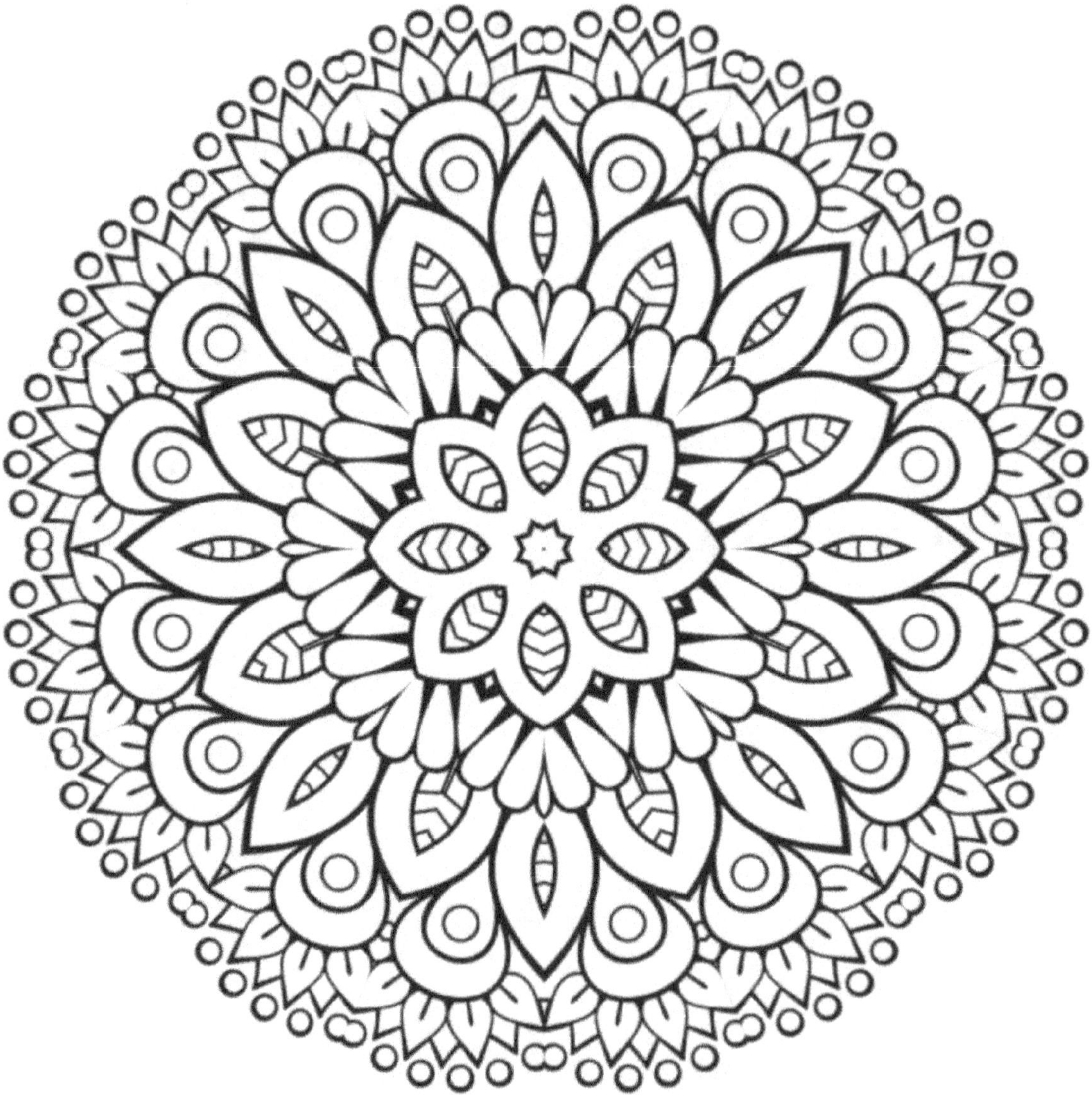

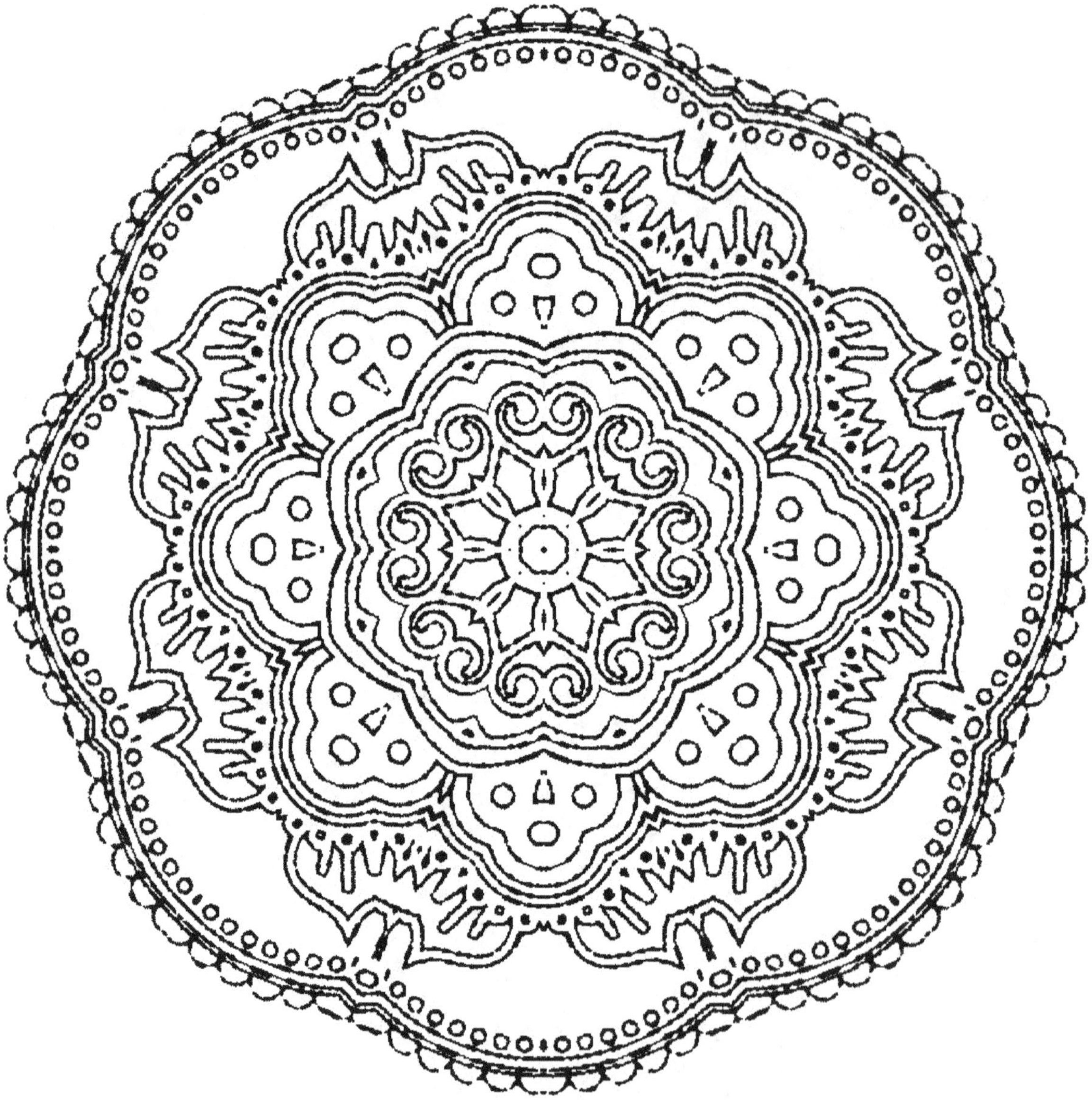

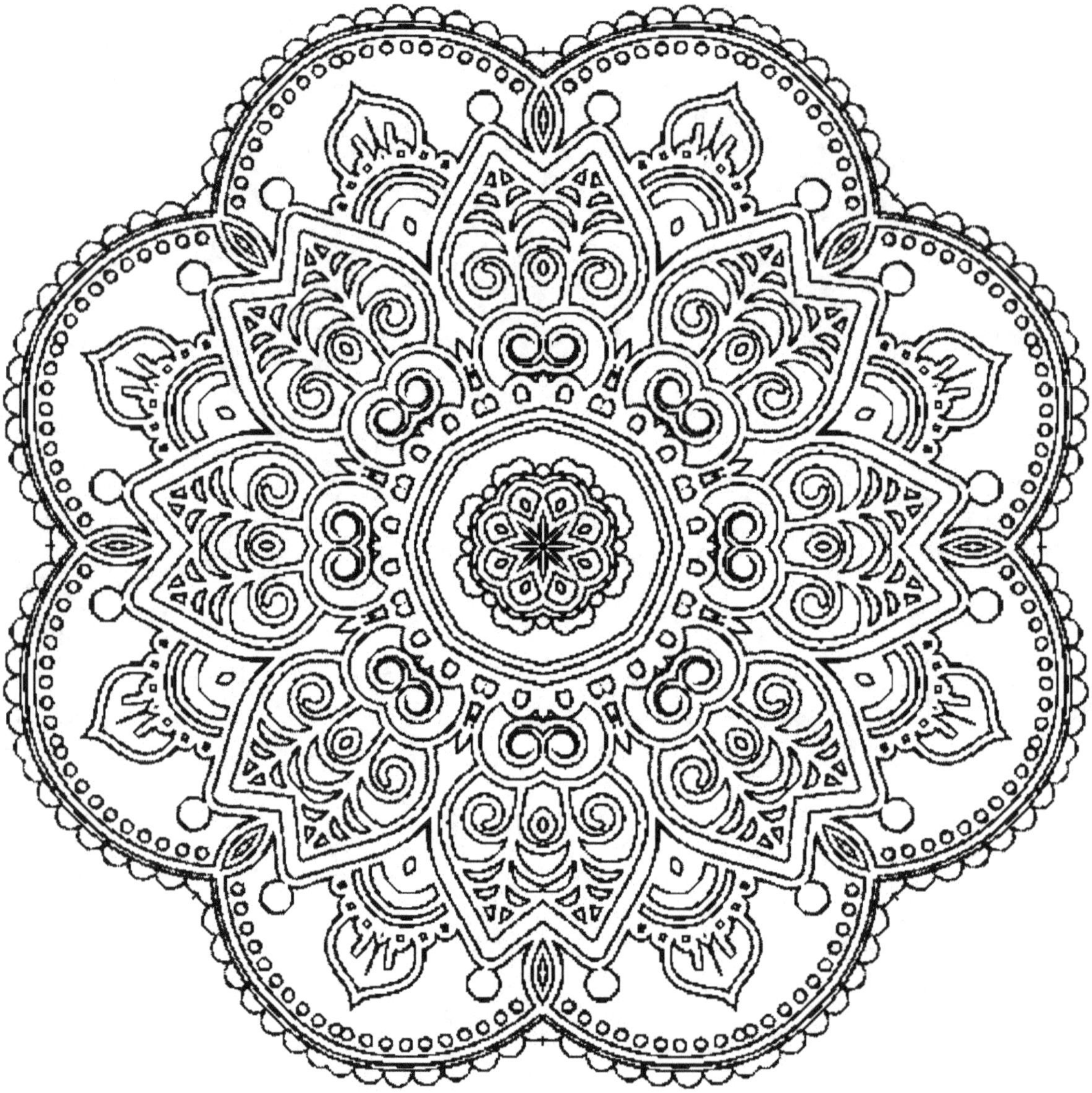

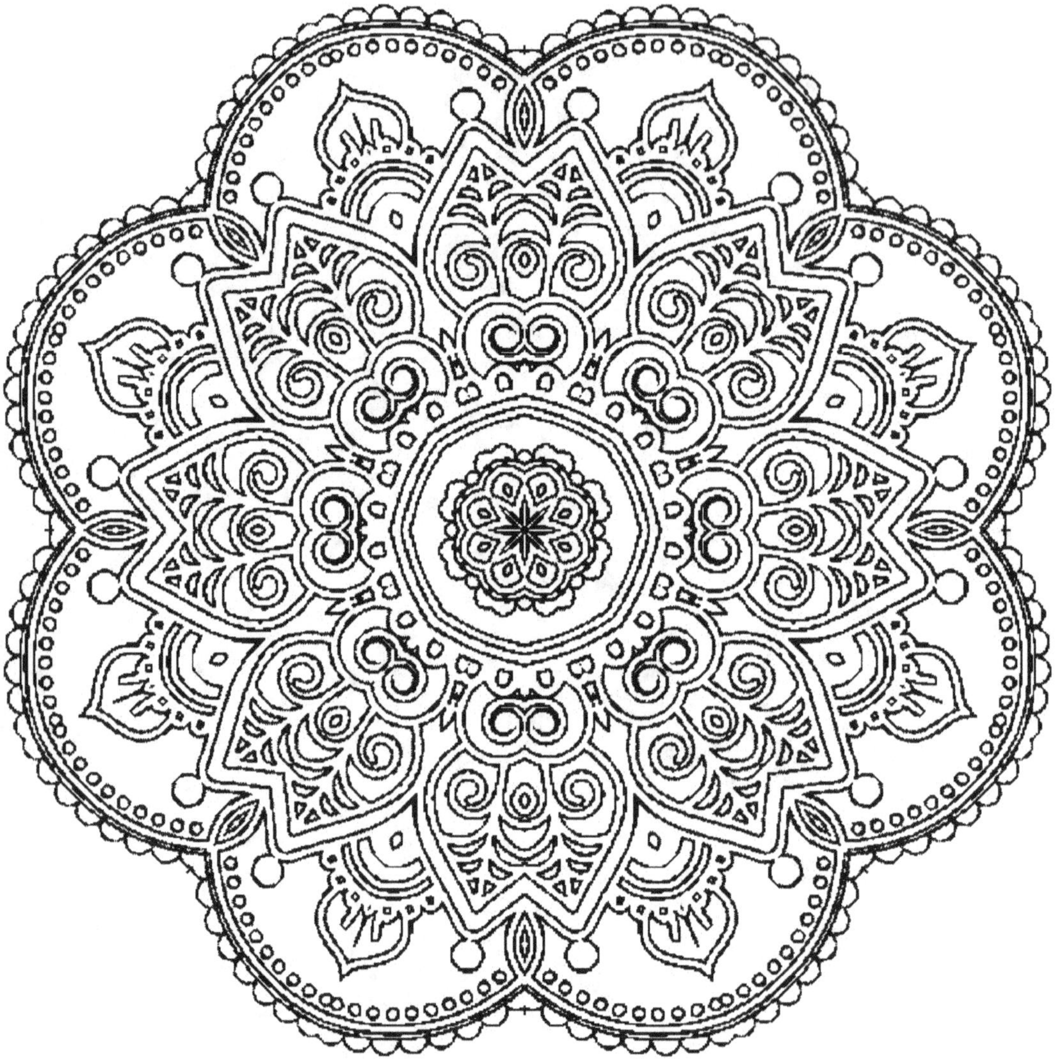

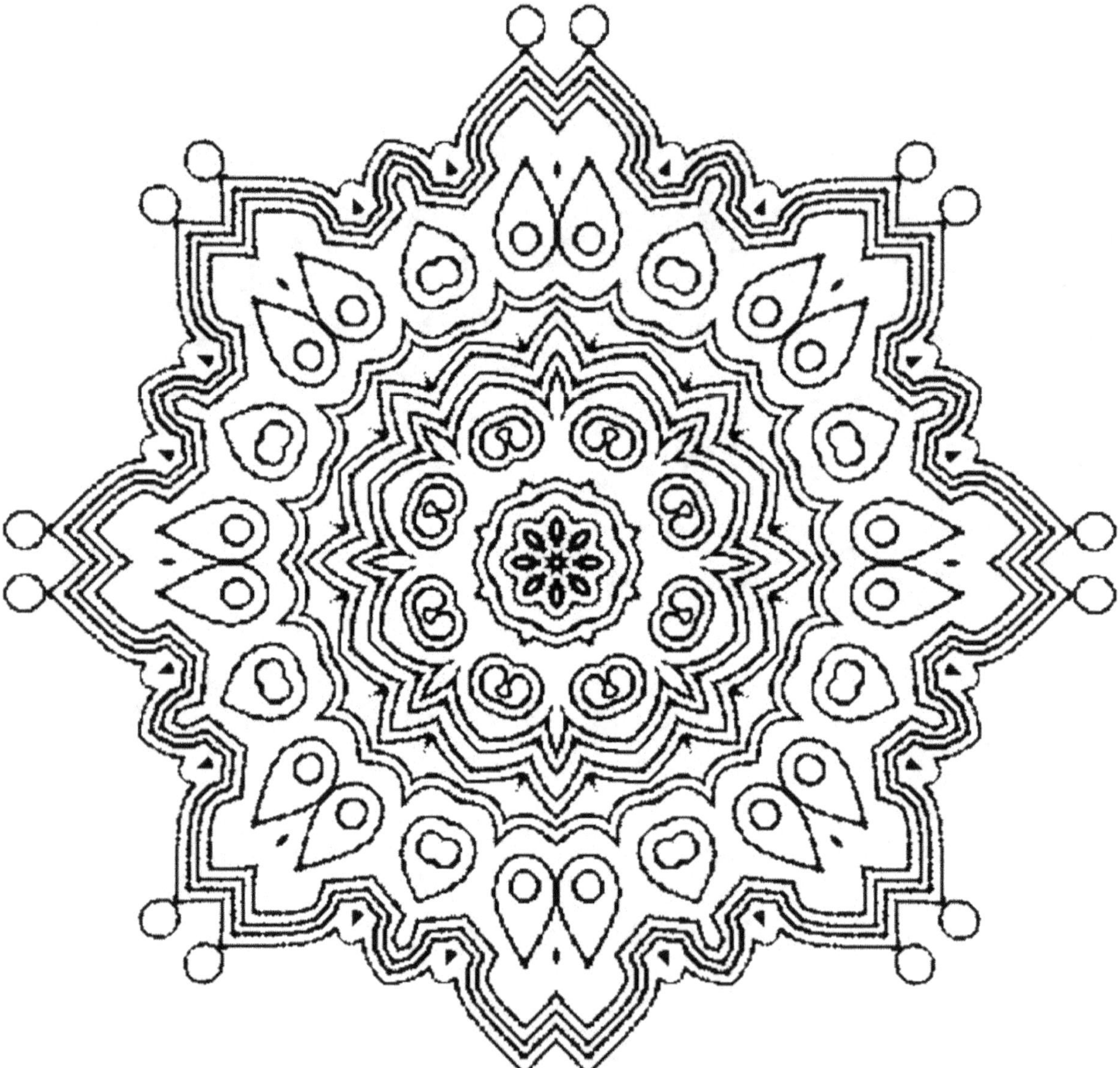

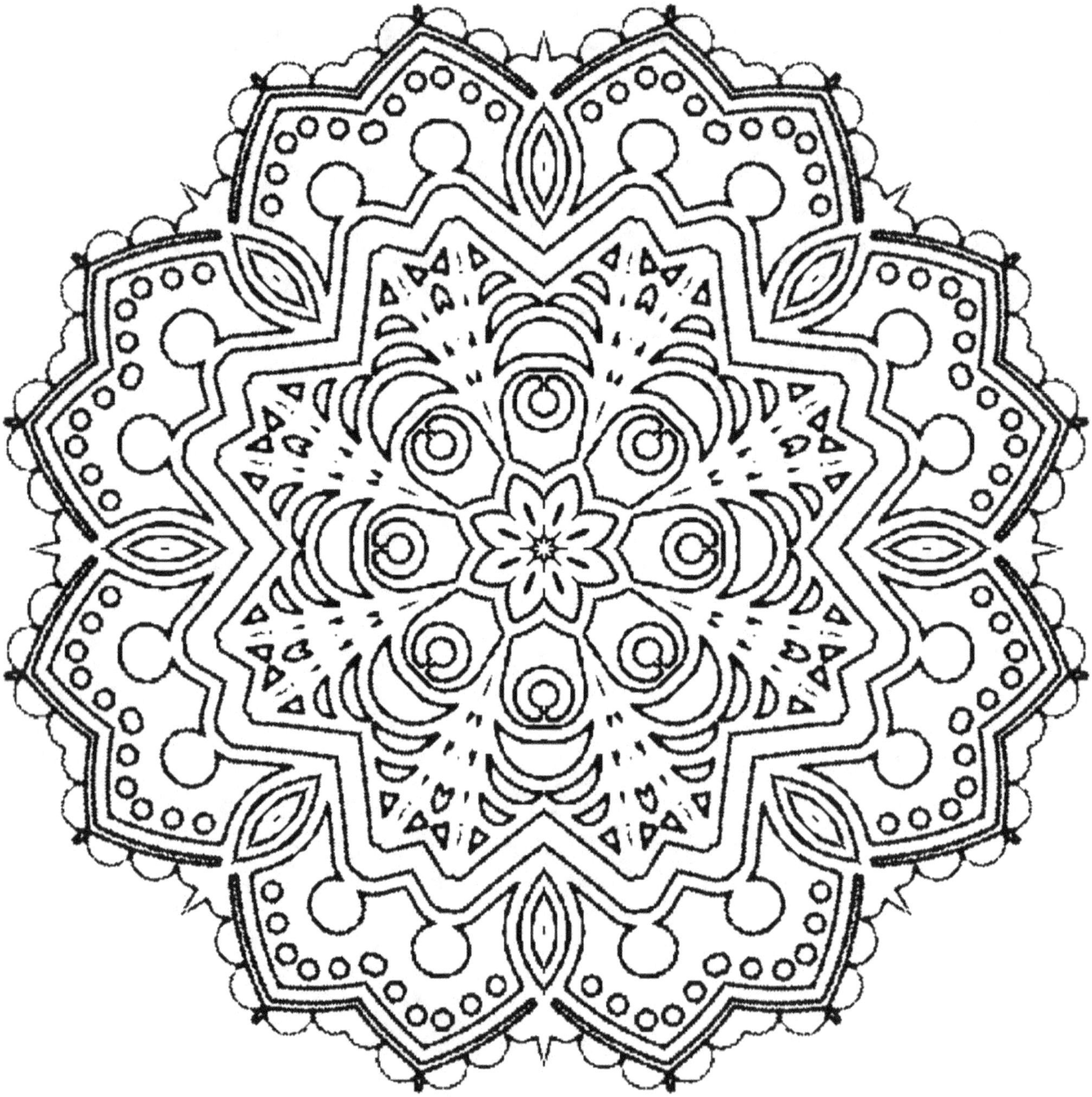

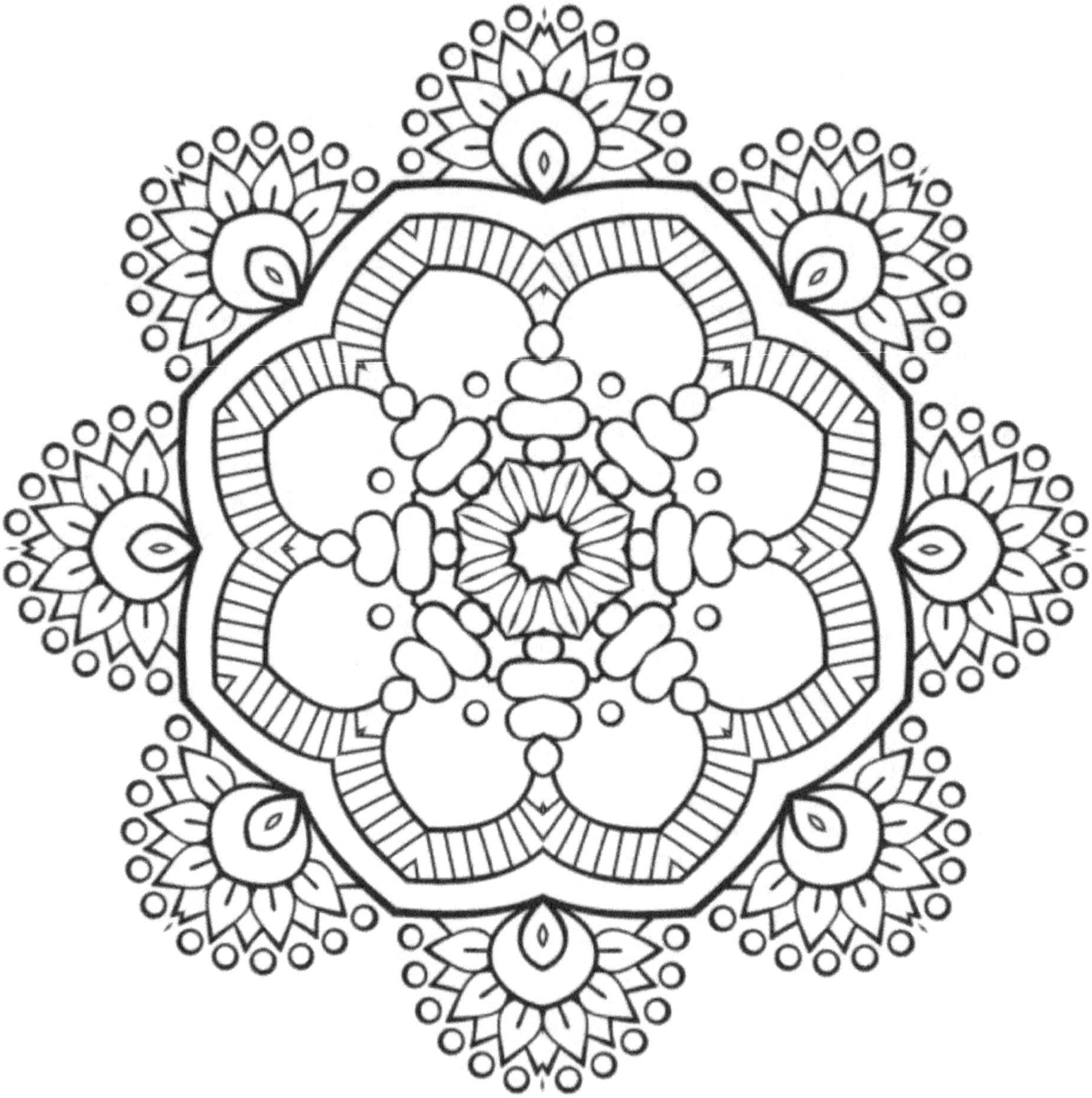

www.ingramcontent.com/pod-product-compliance
Lightning Source LLC
Chambersburg PA
CBHW080818220526
45466CB00011BB/3603
9781686100796